this book belongs to:

_____

I WOULD LIKE TO WHOLEHEARTEDLY EXTEND MY SINCEREST GRATITUDE TO EACH AND EVERY ONE OF YOU FOR BEING AN INTEGRAL PART OF THESE DESIGNS. WITH AN OVERWHELMING SEA OF TITLES AND BOOK CHOICES AVAILABLE, AND SO MANY TALENTED PUBLISHERS TO CHOOSE FROM, YOUR DECISION TO EMBRACE THIS BOOK FILLS MY HEART WITH SUCH GRATITUDE THAT WORDS FAIL TO FULLY CONVEY. THANK YOU! YOUR SUPPORT MEANS THE WORLD!

AS WE BEGAN CREATING THIS SERIES, WE POURED OUR HEARTS AND SOULS INTO EACH PIECE OF ART, METICULOUSLY CRAFTING EVERY PAGE WITH UNWAVERING PASSION. OUR GOAL IS TO CONTINUOUSLY ELEVATE OUR CRAFT, EACH TIME CLOSER AND CLOSER TO THE SUBJECT OF OUR BOOKS.

PLEASE SHARE YOUR REVIEWS ON AMAZON, AS YOUR FEEDBACK FORMS AN INVALUABLE CONNECTION BETWEEN THIS SERIES AND OUR CHERISHED COMMUNITY. YOUR INPUT FUELS THE DRIVE FOR CONSTANT IMPROVEMENT, INSPIRING US TO PRODUCE EVEN MORE CAPTIVATING BOOKS IN THE FUTURE.

CONNECT WITH US ON INSTAGRAM @ENCHANTEDTONES, WHERE I EAGERLY AWAIT GLIMPSES OF YOUR CREATIVE BRILLIANCE REFLECTED IN EACH ILLUSTRATION. DON'T FORGET TO SHARE YOUR CREATIONS USING OUR HASHTAG:

#ENCHANTEDTONES

WE HUMBLY REQUEST YOUR UTMOST RESPECT FOR THE HARD WORK AND DEDICATION INVESTED IN CRAFTING THIS BOOK. NO PART OF THIS PUBLICATION MAY BE REPRODUCED, DISTRIBUTED, OR TRANSMITTED WITHOUT OUR EXPRESS PERMISSION. THIS INCLUDES PHOTOCOPYING, RECORDING, OR ANY OTHER ELECTRONIC OR DIGITAL FORMAT TECHNOLOGY MAY DEVELOP.

IN SIMPLE TERMS, WE KINDLY ASK YOU NOT TO PLAGIARIZE THE WORK. NOT TOO BIG OF AN ASK, RIGHT?

ISBN: 978-65-982085-6-1
PUBLISHED BY: ENCHANTED TONES
COPYRIGHT© 2023 BY ENCHANTED TONES
ALL RIGHTS RESERVED.

"We had the Belle Époque. Now we have the Botox Époque, permeated by plastic emotions from antidepressants and plastic veneers from collagen, silicone, cosmetic surgery and Botox."

— *Maureen Dowd*

Suggested playlist for your coloring experience:

 *Claude Debussy*

Origins

The Belle Époque, with its mixture of optimism, cultural richness, and technological progress, left a lasting impact on European society and culture. It's often looked back on as a kind of golden age.

The Belle Époque, which translates to "Beautiful Era," is generally considered to have spanned from the late 19th century to the outbreak of World War I. Most historians mark its beginning around the 1870s or 1880s, following the end of the Franco-Prussian War in 1871 and the establishment of the Third French Republic.

The end of the Belle Époque is typically placed at the start of World War I in 1914, which brought dramatic changes to the societal and cultural landscape of the world.

Technological Progress

This era was marked by rapid industrial growth and technological innovation. The Second Industrial Revolution was in full swing, leading to advancements in steel production, electricity, and chemical processes. These developments spurred economic growth and urbanization. The introduction of inventions like the telephone, automobile, and cinema revolutionized everyday life and communication. Cities expanded with new infrastructure like subways and electrified street lighting, reflecting a modernizing society.

Cultural Flourishing

The Belle Époque was a golden age for arts and culture. In visual arts, movements like Impressionism and Art Nouveau broke from traditional methods, focusing on light, color, and new forms. Literature saw the rise of naturalism and symbolism. The era also witnessed the birth of modernism in music, with composers experimenting with new harmonic structures. The Parisian cabaret became a symbol of the era's vibrant nightlife and cultural diversity.

Social Changes

Social structures underwent significant changes. The growth of the middle class altered societal dynamics, with increasing emphasis on education and leisure. Women's roles began to shift as well, with early feminist movements advocating for rights like suffrage and better working conditions. However, social disparities were also evident, with stark contrasts between the wealthy elite and the working poor.

Political Stability

Despite underlying tensions, the Belle Époque was a period of relative peace in Europe, especially among major powers. This stability was maintained through a complex network of alliances and treaties. The era also saw the height of European colonial empires, with major powers competing for global influence and resources.

Scientific Advancements

This period was rich in scientific discoveries and innovations. Marie Curie's research on radioactivity and Albert Einstein's early work on the theory of relativity are standout examples. These advancements laid the groundwork for modern physics and had profound implications for the understanding of the natural world.

Expositions and World's Fairs

The Belle Époque is well-known for its grand expositions and world fairs, which were platforms for nations to showcase their cultural and technological achievements. The 1889 Paris Exposition, which introduced the Eiffel Tower, is a notable example. These events were not only displays of national pride but also opportunities for cultural exchange and technological display.

Contrasts

Despite its name, the Belle Époque was not without its problems. The era saw significant social and economic inequalities. The opulence of the upper classes contrasted sharply with the often dismal living and working conditions of the working class. Writers like Émile Zola and Charles Dickens highlighted these social issues in their works, critiquing the inequities of their time.

Fashion

The Belle Époque was a transformative period for fashion, reflecting the era's broader cultural and social changes. The fashion of the period is often remembered for its distinctive silhouettes. Women's fashion featured the S-bend corset, which pushed the chest forward and the hips back, creating an S-shaped figure. This silhouette was a departure from the previously popular hourglass shape. Skirts were flared and gored, and by the end of the era, began to show a narrower line. High collars and "leg of mutton" sleeves were also characteristic of the period.

Haute Couture

The Belle Époque was a significant era for the development of haute couture, especially in Paris, which became the fashion capital of the world. Designers like Charles Frederick Worth, known as the father of haute couture, played a pivotal role in shaping fashion. Worth was the first to present seasonal collections to clients and is credited with moving fashion towards the modern industry it is today.

Technological Impact on Fashion

Advances in textile production and dyeing techniques greatly influenced fashion. There was an increased availability of fabrics like silk and velvet, and the use of synthetic dyes brought new, vibrant colors into vogue. The sewing machine, which became widely used during this period, also revolutionized how clothes were made, making them more accessible to a broader public.

Art and Culture

Art movements like Art Nouveau influenced fashion, with clothing and accessories featuring curvilinear designs, floral motifs, and intricate details. The influence of Japanese art, which became popular in Europe during this time, could also be seen in fabrics and designs.

Accessories

: Accessories were an essential part of Belle Époque fashion. Women wore gloves, hats, and elaborate hairstyles adorned with combs and pins. Jewelry was lavish, with chokers (called dog collars), brooches, and long necklaces being particularly fashionable.

Simplicity

Towards the end of the Belle Époque, fashion began to shift towards simpler and more practical styles. This change was partly influenced by the growing women's suffrage movement and the onset of World War I, which demanded more functional clothing.

ENCHANTED
TONES